Beautiful
California Coast

Beautiful
California Coast

Text by Paul M. Lewis

Library of Congress Cataloging in Publication Data
Lewis, Paul M.
   Beautiful California Coast.
    1. California—Description and travel—1951—Views.
    2. Coasts—California—Pictorial works.
I. Title.
F862.L54   917.94   79-13134
ISBN 0-915796-97-X (hardbound)
ISBN 0-915796-96-1 (paperback)

First Printing May 1979

Published by Beautiful America Publishing Company
P.O. Box 608, Beaverton, Oregon 97005
Robert D. Shangle, Publisher

PHOTO CREDITS

WAYNE ALDRIDGE—*page 50.*

ROY BISHOP—*page 11, above; page 15, below; page 18; page 19, below; page 20, below; page 24, below; page 28, below; page 29; page 37, above; page 40, above; page 41; page 43, below; page 52; page 53, below; page 56, above; page 65, below.*

JAMES BLANK—*page 28, above.*

ED COOPER—*page 11, below; page 22; page 23, below; page 60, above; page 69.*

JOHN GRONERT—*pages 32-33; page 51, below; page 55, above; page 72.*

JOHN HILL—*page 9; page 10; pages 12-13; page 14; pages 16-17; page 21; page 25; page 42; page 54; page 55, below; page 57; page 64.*

TOM MYERS—*page 47, below; page 65, above.*

C.W. PENTICOFF—*page 24, above.*

MIKE RIZZO JR.—*page 36.*

ROBERT SHANGLE—*page 15, above; page 19, above; page 20, above; page 23, above; page 40, below; page 43, above; page 46; page 47, above; pages 48-49; page 51, above; page 53, above; page 60, below; page 61; page 68.*

BRUCE and SAM WHITE—*page 37, below; page 56, below.*

Lithography by Fremont Litho Inc., Fremont, California

CONTENTS

The Coast of Many Colors

Everyone knows how exciting the California shoreline is. Hard sell is quite unnecessary to attract visitors. But the parts that get visited the most are only a small share of its twelve-hundred-mile length. The southern crescent from Long Beach to San Diego represents in many minds the only coast there is. Nothing can beat sand, surf, and sun, if they show up in the proper proportions. The marvelous golden beaches of Southern California attract the public in unbelievable hordes on a pleasant summer weekend, which makes the beach situation a little less pleasant for each individual member of those mobs. But what can you expect? The beaches are handy to the great population centers.

If the southern beaches are smothering under the weight of the adoring multitudes, the northern shore is comparatively unvisited. Yet it is one of the world's most dramatic, where sea and land meet in spectacular confrontation. Nature has not yet given it over to man; wildlife is so abundant you would think they owned the earth. From Monterey northward great bays and peninsulas define its profile. Sun, rain, summer fogs, and violent tides make up its varying moods. Its gigantic headlands drop abruptly into the ocean as if surprised by the proximity of the waves. Offshore rocks and pinnacles rise heavily out of the salt spray like some immense monsters left over from another age. Sometimes the fogs and mists displace their outlines so that they seem to move.

Some of the far north coast of California is so remote and isolated it doesn't seem to fit in as a part of the nation's most populous state. Things are done here the same way they have been done for years. Ranchlands and dairy farms cover the coastal hills and mountain slopes. Big fleets of commercial and charter fishing boats crowd the harbors that are big enough to receive them. Lumber, although somewhat diminished, still rules the roost. Life is harder, but simpler, on the north coast; the sea is a harsh overlord here, sometimes going into tearing rages that work a great hardship on those who live near it and depend on it for their livelihood.

This collection of landscape closeups samples many aspects of California's coast from border to border. The beauty is both obvious and subtle, sometimes quite unbelievable. We have seized the moment, sometimes, when the elements are at their harshest. We have, to complete the portrait, found the sea and the shore merged in the gentlest of embraces. We think you will like this album on the California coast, and for another reason than just the pure pleasure of looking at creative nature photography. Our pictures are exquisite proof that the original is still there, in much the same great shape as it has been ever since it became a coastline. The heavy tread of human multitudes may be putting parts of it to the ultimate test of strength, but so far that green and golden shore has withstood the challenge.

PML

The Mountains and the Sea

San Francisco and its Bay occupy a separate universe from all other earthly locales, so for that reason, if no other, they are outside the limits of this commentary. However, the Bay Area is a convenient doorway between north and south coasts. To the north of the Golden Gate is mountainous, peninsular Marin County. Most of the Golden Gate National Recreation Area is on the north side, encompassing the Marin Headlands, an area long closed to public access. The steep ocean side once belonged to the Army and the rest was in private hands. Down the cliffs from State Highway 1 (the Shoreline Highway) are some famous and popular beaches, such as Muir and Stinson. The town of Bolinas anchors the southern corner of big, triangle-shaped Point Reyes National Seashore, the single most prominent feature of the Marin coastline. Point Reyes extends out into the ocean from a wide base with Bolinas on the south and Tomales Point on the north.

The *Punta de los Reyes* is a wild, hilly promontory that acquired its name, "Point of Kings," from the Spanish explorer Sebastian Vizcaino, who sighted it in 1603. Formerly private ranch and dairy lands, Point Reyes is now a primitive reserve that provides permanent habitat for hundreds of bird and mammal species and temporary quarters for migratory types, including hikers and backpackers. Point Reyes used to have its share of grizzlies, too, and elk, but those animals went when the settlers came in the early nineteenth century. Now an attempt is being made to introduce tule elk, an endangered species. The grizzlies may have to wait.

The peninsula is quite literally a separate world. The huge triangle of rocky promontory is almost an island, separated from the Marin mainland by the San Andreas fault running along the eastern base. Point Reyes is just a visitor at its present location, traveling along the coast at a rate of two inches a year. Fascinated geologists have discovered that the composition of its granite base is different from the Marin coast rocks east of the fault line. Point Reyes is believed to have moved up the coast to its present latitude from the southern part of the Sierra Nevada, where it was formed forty million years ago.

Whatever its age and transient nature, Point Reyes is 100 square miles of lonely beaches and white-chalk cliffs, hilly pasturelands, and forested coastal mountains. The National Seashore portion comprises 64,000 acres and has 70 miles of coastline. There are a few roads on the peninsula, mostly in the northern portion where some

Continued on page 26

(Preceding page) For centuries pounding waves have shaped these arches at Pt. Lobos, south of Carmel.

(Opposite) Plume grass stands in evening's stillness where the Russian River enters the sea.

(Right) Hardy and curious gulls are found everywhere on the California coast.

(Below) The gentle climate around Pacific Grove encourages abundant floral growth like the yellow cone flowers in the foreground.

(Following pages) Sun, mist, stone and the mighty ocean produce intriguing vistas along the Big Sur coastline.

(Second following page) The day's work done, fishing boats rest at anchor in the harbor at Bodega Bay.

(Preceding page, above) The "retired" lighthouse at Point Loma, now part of Cabrillo National Monument in San Diego, stands in stark whiteness against the colorful flora of the cape.

(Preceding page, below) Low but rocky headlands are punctuated by small intimate beaches along much of the Sonoma County coastline.

(Left) Evening sun adds a rosy and golden tone to the rocky shoreline north of Mendocino.

(Following page) A spectacular sunset may be the reward of an evening spent on Carmel's 17-Mile Drive.

(Second following page, above) The setting sun puts Lombard Street in deep shadow while still lighting North Beach and distant Coit Tower in this late-evening view of San Francisco.

(Second following page, below) Sea arches at Santa Cruz frame a man-made development on the bluffs in the background.

(Left) Colorful California poppies, familiar and easy to identify, are the most plentiful wildflower along the coast.

(Below) The glowering cliffs in Mendocino Headlands State Park tower over the waters that sculpted their rugged forms.

(Opposite) The surf laps peacefully on this broad sweep of sandy beach at Patrick's Point, near Trinidad.

(Following page) Brilliant wildflowers highlight the rugged flanks of Pt. Reyes at the Pt. Reyes National Seashore.

(Second following page, above) Drifting fog wraps the Big Sur coastline in mystery.

(Second following page, below) The coast highway follows the Big Sur shoreline, carved out of the looming headlands high above the water.

(Third following page, above) Rosy-golden sunset throws the Golden Gate Bridge and Marin headlands into sharp relief as a jogger and friend enjoy a solitary evening run along the shore of San Francisco Bay.

(Third following page, below) Breakers roll across this solitary expanse of beach near Trinidad.

cattle ranching and dairy farming is still permitted. The National Park Service has established an extensive trail system leading to wilderness areas, such as Drake's Bay on the south.

The peninsula is shrouded in fog—the real pea-soup stuff—much of the year. But its temperatures are in the mild range, varying but a few degrees through the seasons. Its bays and bluffs, lakes and marshes, sand dunes and prairies, and coniferous forests are a micro-universe of plant and animal life. Even the eagle and mountain lion find a home here. Some of the other residents are herons, hawks, falcons, foxes, badgers, rabbits, bobcats, and deer. The waters and tidal flats on and around Point Reyes are aswarm with fresh and saltwater fish, and shellfish.

Tomales Bay, which cuts 16 narrow miles into the peninsula from the north, is on the lee side of Inverness Ridge, which keeps out the winds and the fogs. The bay's sheltered beaches provide the bathing and swimming ambiance missing from the peninsula's stormy sea-girt coast.

The next northern coastal county is Sonoma. Bereft of harbors except for Bodega Bay, Sonoma has nonetheless natural and historical features that make it an extremely attractive 40 miles. It's the "Russian" coast, with inland valleys farmed by Russian colonists in the early nineteenth century. The Russian-American Fur Company, chartered by Catherine the Great, was then based in Sitka, whence came Ivan Alexander Kussoff to build a port (Romanoff), a town (Kussoff), and a stockade (at Fort Ross). Today, the Shoreline Highway (California 1) swerves away from the steep coastline north of Tomales Bay and rolls through hilly woods and meadows that were farmed by the Russians for 30 years, until they left in 1841. The coast road gets back by the sea at the village of Bodega Bay and its harbor. The town owes its appearance more to New England influences than Russian ones, situated as it is on the steep slopes of a mountain that plunge abruptly into the harbor. Bodega Harbor is shallow, edged with salt marshes and tidal flats, and running back to a shoreline that provides an environment for a wide range of wildlife. And in such waters the invertebrates flourish like ants at a picnic—there are many varieties of shrimp, crab, and clams. The natural conditions are just right for this explosion of life offshore and on. The only present scarcity is of genus *homo*, which possibly helps all the other life forms to reach their astonishing populations.

The coast road stays near the shoreline for a long haul now, hanging onto bluffs that drop steeply to the beach. From Bodega Bay to the Russian River, about 15 miles, are a whole string of state beaches under the aegis of Sonoma Coast State

(Preceding page) A lone fishing boat bobs in the deep waters south of Carmel Highlands, as gentle waves break on the shoreline's rockiness.

Beach. These are not swimming beaches, unless you are a sea lion. The surf is too cold and stormy. But fishermen prowl the sands and skin divers slip in under the rocky ledges, for surf smelt on the one hand and abalone on the other. Just plain nature lovers enjoy the delicious intimacy of the private little coves, hidden from the road above them by the steep cliffs.

The Russian River brings a different look to the coastal vicinity, both by the configuration of its setting and the crowds of fishermen periodically lured to its estuary by the promise of steelhead and perch. The river's canyon cuts through the mountains, leading inland to one of the rare areas of dense population on the coast and after a few miles reaches one of the most heavily used resort areas on the north coast, filled with everything to make life pleasant in the not-so-wild woods. There are swimming and boating beaches, lodges, campsites, and restaurants in and around the communities along the river's redwood-lined banks. The centerpiece of all this is Guerneville, in an area that not only epitomizes the beauty of the Russian River region, but attracts persons of every economic level and philosophical persuasion.

Another of California's priceless remaining groves of big trees is three miles north of Guerneville. Armstrong Redwoods State Reserve has been a state park since 1934 and is quite primitive, except for a small campground inside its northern boundary. This reserve is a modest 440 acres, but connects by a narrow road to the much more extensive Austin Creek State Recreation Area, whose 4,300 acres are mostly wilderness, with trails only.

Back on the coast, things have become straight up and down. Between Russian Gulch and Fort Ross the mountains have moved in and usurped the place where the beach should be. The road clings to the steep shoulders for dear life, the ocean side sometimes plunging straight down. The highway does a series of contortions to enable it to follow the coast profile, then arrives at Fort Ross. The stockade again looks the way it did when the Russians were in residence. The big Salt Point State Park (3,500 acres to the north) occupies the shoreline for six miles, reaching up onto the high ridge on the east. Salt Point has tide pool areas that are protected as a state reserve. The ocean frontage is often quite sheer, but there are coves and ledges that are ideal for surf casting and diving for abalone. Next door to Salt Point is the Kruse Rhododendron State Reserve. The best time to be on the trails is when the rhodys are blooming in May.

(Following page, above) Brightly-colored catamarans are beached on the shore of San Diego's Mission Bay, waiting for a breeze and some passengers.
(Following page, below) Mountains sit back a short way from the sea on the coastline south of Big Sur.

Stewarts Point, a relic of a town, makes an appearance of sorts a few miles north. Early in this century it was a busy lumber port of the ''doghole'' kind. Ships were loaded offshore by means of a wooden chute which leaned out over the water. It was a chancy business, because a ship could easily run up on the reefs during loading. In rough weather such accidents were hard to avoid.

The seashore is blocked for most of the next 14 miles by a private development known as Sea Ranch, a ''city'' with a potential population of 50,000. The project, so far, has been carried out with extreme care for the surroundings, but it cuts off public beach access.

One of the coast's lovely rivers, the Gualala, comes into the picture after Sea Ranch. It introduces the Mendocino Coast, 120 miles of varied and mysterious shoreline. Gualala, the town, began in the 1860s as another of those tiny lumber ports; it now turns its attention to art and tourism. The seascape is very productive of fine views in this vicinity, with bluffs and headlands and fringes of forest reaching down from the higher hills. The big promontory of Point Arena is largely rolling pasture, devoted to dairy herds. The mountains stand back a way, leaving more open space for the fields and a town. The community—Point Arena—is a quiet little place that used to be one of the north coast's bigger lumber ports, as well as a stop for passenger ships. There is still a wharf, now little used except in summer by commercial salmon boats. There is also a tall lighthouse on the point, with the most powerful beacon on the coast, visible 21 miles out to sea.

The Navarro River, one of the bigger coastal streams, comes through the mountains six miles to the north, after having traversed the interior Coast Range. State Highway 128 follows the Navarro Valley to some redwood groves and a couple of state-park campgrounds along the stream.

The Navarro, the Garcia to the south, and the Noyo to the north are extremely beautiful wilderness rivers where canoe float trips provide the ultimate in peace and solitude. Whereas much of the land is tied up in private hands, the rivers belong to everyone and can be traveled freely. The only limitation is the amount of stream flow, which drops during the summer to the point where the rivers are no longer navigable. The only exceptions to this are the very biggest rivers, such as the Eel, the Smith, and the Russian.

A cluster of state parks decorates the next few coastal miles. Van Damme is the southernmost, noteworthy because of its pygmy forest of cypress and Bolander pines, trees whose development has been stunted by having to grow in a shallow, whitish topsoil leached of some essential chemicals by heavy rains and having a hardpan subsoil

(Preceding page) A lone sunset-watcher stands under the looming rocks at Aliso Beach.

30

resistant to root penetration. These particular soil conditions occur in patches, so that the pygmies grow right alongside the coast's normal-sized trees. Van Damme is on the landward side of the highway, and stretches five miles into the hills, with a lushly beautiful fern canyon taking up some of that length. About twenty miles inland, at the same latitude as Van Damme, is one of the most impressive redwood forests left in the state: Montgomery Woods State Reserve, a wilderness accessible only by an unpaved road that takes off from the Shoreline Highway and climbs over the coast hills. It, too, has a mossy-green canyon where ferns grow to giant proportions.

Mendocino City, next up on the coast, fits into its coastal environment in a way that could be a model for human communities. The town is planted on a headland forming the north shore of Mendocino Bay, and fairly exudes atmosphere, in the best sense. Its appearance is typical of the antique New England look of several north coast towns. But more than that, its carefully preserved past has been brought to bear on the realities of today, woven into the community's concern for the individual and his right to a quality life. Mendocino was once one of those big lumber ports, a hard-working town whose glory came from braving the stormy seas to get the lumber shipped out. The community still has the look of a place that has struggled to live its own life.

State preserves established around Mendocino have been crucial to the persistence of the simple life and rustic look of the town. Mendicino Headlands State Park takes in the sea cliffs and the Big River beaches that border the town. Two miles north is Russian Gulch State Park, running up into the hills from the seashore, as Van Damme park does. A shoreside road from Russian Gulch leads past Point Cabrillo to nearby Caspar Headlands State Reserve and Beach.

The indented coastline of the Fort Bragg area is a visual excitement that is best seen from the deck of an offshore boat, such as a fishing charter. The road is no help here; the coastal profile is hidden from it much of the way. But there are other aspects of this coast worth investigating. One of the attractions is Jackson State Forest, reached by State Highway 20 out of Noyo. Certain areas of the forest are set aside for deer hunters during the season. Certain other areas are used as an experimental forest, where the effects of logging on erosion and stream siltation are studied.

A spectacular river-ocean tableau appears just north of the Highway 20 junction at the Noyo River estuary, a fjord-like inlet crossed by the coast road. The harbor shelters swarms of fishing boats and offers tourist and marine-related businesses. Highway travelers get a thrilling bird's eye view of the bay, the harbor, and the village from the high bridge that takes the coast road over the river and on to Fort Bragg. Fort Bragg is a big town by north coast standards. It counts about 5,000

(Left) A little creek makes a spectacular high-dive to join the ocean in this rocky Big Sur cove.

residents, many of whom run businesses having to do with traveling and with the needs of the fishing fraternity. Fort Bragg began in 1857 as a true fort, built to control the many different Indian tribes of the Mendocino Reservation. The fort and reservation were abandoned a few years later when the redwood forests of the area began to look attractive to lumber interests; the town of Fort Bragg started life in earnest in 1889, and is still primarily a mill town.

The passenger train is alive and well in Fort Bragg. The "Skunk" railroad climbs up the Noyo River canyon for 40 miles to Willits, over a route of high trestles and tricky hairpin curves. What started as a logging railroad, following the woods crews early in the century, became a regular passenger line (the California Western Railroad) when it was completed to Willits in 1911 and linked to the Northwestern Pacific. Round trips are made daily to Willits through the magnificent river and forest scenery, stopping often to let off hikers and campers, deliver supplies and mail to wood dwellers, and pick up whoever or whatever can be accommodated. In summer, an extra train, the "Super Skunk," is added to the run, with a real-live steam engine pulling it.

The Shoreline Highway north of Fort Bragg touches one of the prize parks in the California system. MacKerricher State Park is reached on a road out of Cleone, a few buildings on the main highway that didn't make it as a town when logging activity moved elsewhere. What is so great about MacKerricher is not its size particularly (1,000 acres), but its variety. It has a long-running beach, with level sand and dunes; the beach ends at a good fishing stream (Ten Mile River); south of the beach are mini-beaches with tide pools, driftwood, agates, and rocky outcroppings; there is a small freshwater lake where motorless boating can be enjoyed while fishing for trout; pine forests and meadows within the park shelter deer, quail, and campers. Next to the park is a wetland (Inglenook Fen) with an ecosystem unique on the California coast; indeed, it is claimed to have life forms found nowhere else in the world.

The long, lonely shoreline for 30 miles and more beyond Fort Bragg has been called the forgotten coast. It was once very active and important in human affairs. Relics are left from towns that in the early days were very much in the center of coastal lumber operations. Other once-booming settlements have disappeared completely. Westport is still a name on the map 16 miles north of Fort Bragg. A gas station and a few houses are all that remain of the time when it was a big lumber shipping port (it once had 14 saloons.)

The adventurous Shoreline Highway gives it up at this point and swerves inland to join up with US 101 at Leggett. But for the last twenty miles or so of Mendocino County and on into Humboldt, an unpaved rural byway takes up the task of following

34

what measures out to the most primitive piece of the north coast. Only a very informal roadway could be expected to keep going when the terrain ahead turns from horizontal to perpendicular.

The route that continues the coastal odyssey is called the Usal Road. It seems to climb into the mountains with the assurance of a road that has been around for awhile. It has. The Usal Road was a part of the on-and-off system connecting the north with the Bay Area before the Redwood Highway was completed in the twenties. It's a thrill a minute driving the Usal Road and connecting byways that climb over and around the King Range. The grades are steep, the curves incredible. But the surface is pretty decent, depending on the season and the frequency of county grading jobs. This is marvelous hiking country, providing the hiker has obtained permission to cross the mostly private domains in his path. The view can be spectacular from the road as it rounds a high cliff that drops off sharply into the surf. But the forest often effectively blocks a view of the extraordinary oceanic setting: foaming breakers, indented shoreline, and misty outlines of rocky offshore islands.

The ocean-facing slopes of the King Range up to the crest are maintained in a wilderness condition by the Bureau of Land Management, which oversees a large share of the range's 54,000 acres. Being an actual part of the coastline, the Kings share in the north coast's fog and wind, especially during the summer. But hikers on the higher elevations can get above the fog, into a world that becomes an enchanted island in the sky. A springtime hiker may even be granted a completely clear day, in which case the coastline panorama will provide a different kind of enchantment.

Shelter Cove, on the coast at the southern end of the range, is one of the few "improvements" until the neighborhood of Eureka. That's about eighty miles of unalloyed nature. Shelter Cove was once occupied by the Sinkyone tribe of the Athabascan Indians. Later, as a community of settlers, it was a lumber and produce port for sailing schooners. Shelter Cove is protected by Point Delgada, whose shallows are rich fishing waters for king and silver salmon. The fine beaches of the bay are diversely interesting. There are tide pools on the rocky parts; clams, driftwood, and agates on the sandy parts. It's one of those "special places" being considered for a state park.

Cape Mendocino is doubtless one of the coast's best advertised landmarks, possibly because it sticks out into the Pacific farther than any other part of the continent south of Alaska. The cape has figured in the journals of the early seaborne explorers such as Cabrillo and Drake, and reefs around it have been responsible for a lot of shipwrecks during the last century and this one. The heart of the Cape

(Following page) Afternoon sunlight touches the layered rock wall with color on this deserted California beach.

35

Mendocino bulge is both primitive and pastoral. But there are roads on it here and there. One of these comes up from the Mattole River and skirts the very tip of the cape itself. The river, the sheep and cattle ranchlands, and the brushy hills make an idyllic approach to the cape's coastal landmarks, such as Sugarloaf Island, rising 300 feet out of the sea just off land's end like a gigantic point of emphasis.

Back of the north Mendocino coast, on the plain of the Eel River delta, are a few towns quite small in size but large in charm. They date from the middle of the last century and stand on bottom-land that once held thick forests of redwoods. Ferndale is one of the best known and best looking of these communities. It has moved into the present with much of its Victorian architectural heritage intact. Highway 101 comes barreling out to Humboldt Bay here, and many of the other pioneer communities are lined up alongside of it. Back roads along forested ridges of the coastal mountains provide scenic links between them.

Big Humboldt Bay is still a natural beauty despite the emphatic presence of Eureka on its shores. The bay is 14 miles long and as much as 3.5 miles wide; much of its shoreline remains innocent of man's alterations and installations. The Humboldt Bay National Wildlife Refuge was established on the South Bay in 1971, taking in some areas of the North Bay in addition. Two slender fingers of sand separate the bay from the ocean, except for a narrow channel that in the past has proved a treacherous passage for ships. Long jetties on the north and south approaches now make movment in and out of the bay a much safer proposition.

Eureka has no exclamation point after it. Too bad. *Eureka*! is, after all, a Greek exclamation, meaning ''I have found it!'' You couldn't really miss it, because the town is the biggest on the north coast (about 24,500 residents). It was started as a lumber town in 1850 and still is heavily involved in the processing and shipping of lumber. Eureka has a big commercial fishing fleet, too; fish canning is another big business here. One of the reminders of Eureka's extravagant past is its most celebrated residence, the ornate Carson Mansion, built in 1886 by lumber mogul William Carson. It has more exterior trim than a sultan's palace in the *Thousand and One Arabian Nights*.

Just up the road from Eureka is Arcata, once a rival to the bigger community for dominance in the area. But Eureka, better situated on the bay for deep-draft vessels, took the lead when lumber eased out mining as the area's primary livelihood. Arcata, however, is the seat of a big university—Humboldt State—that concerns itself with

(Preceding page, above) Pleasure craft fill the slips at Dana Point Harbor, south of Laguna.

(Preceding page, below) The hills break abruptly as they meet the ocean along this stretch of San Mateo County shoreline, just north of San Gregorio.

oceanography and the fishing and forestry industries. North from Arcata the Redwood Highway becomes a shore road, albeit freeway-sized. The ocean is right there for most of the way, either snuggled up to the freeway or to pieces of old Highway 101 that have been bypassed. The bypassed road is more scenic, and the slower pace on it makes the scenery more visible.

Trinidad Head and its harbor are the focus of several coastal features beginning about twelve miles north of Arcata. First up are two spots popular with clam diggers—Clam Beach and, nearby, Little River State Beach, bounded on the north by Little River. Trinidad is high and mighty for a little town. It perches on a coastal bluff and might be excused for looking down on other north-coast towns because it is officially the oldest (incorporated in 1852). It actually does look down on a little harbor that is both snug and spectacular. Big, bulbous Trinidad Head protects the port from summer northwesterlies, looming importantly over the little pleasure craft that share space with lesser rocks scattered like so many of the big headland's progeny. Very close by is another of those agate beaches, this one at Patrick's Point State Park.

An area of coastal lagoons begins a couple of miles north of the park and extends nine miles along the low shoreline. Formerly saltwater bays, the lagoons gradually evolved into shallow freshwater lakes when their openings to the sea were closed off by the buildup of low sand dikes. During the winter rains the lagoons overflow into the Pacific, permitting the entry of ocean fish such as flounder, salmon, and steelhead. The biggest is called, appropriately, Big Lagoon. It's four miles long, 19 feet deep and 2,000 acres in extent. Others in the series are Dry Lagoon, a small marshy area; Stone Lagoon, and Freshwater Lagoon. Parts of their shorelines are incorporated into county and state preserves. The Three Lagoons Recreation Area, a lumber company's private preserve, takes in the east shores and is open to the public.

The remaining sixty miles or so of California's north coast concentrate the biggest redwood parks in what might be called—to use a musical analogy—a paramount ending. Three state preserves have been combined into Redwood National Park. Although the national park is still more a name than an accomplished fact, eventually it will become a fully functional unit of the federal system. The present three state parks—Prairie Creek, Del Norte, and Jedediah Smith—didn't just happen. Conservationists began organizing the purchase of land early in the century,

Continued on page 58

(Following page, above) Mountains rise sharply behind the storm-swept Crescent City lighthouse, enjoying a moment's calm on a sunny evening.
(Following page, below) A nearly-deserted north coast beach tempts strollers where a tiny stream joins the sea.

(Preceding page) Water and sand seem turned to gold as day ends at Aliso Beach.

(Opposite) The lighthouse on Point Arena flashes its warning miles out to sea.

(Right) Brilliant flowers of many varieties enjoy the mild climate and great growing conditions along the California coast.

(Below) A powerful surf at Mendocino State Park displays the great force that sculpts the picturesque rock formations.

(Following pages) The tortured lines of this lone, weatherbeaten cypress etch themselves sharply against the rosy hues of day's last light.

(Opposite) These ocean-sculpted rocks testify to the power of the waves along the Big Sur Coast.

(Right) The mild coastal climate is great for flower gardens—and honeybees!

(Below) Morro Rock looms in the background while sandpipers search the shallows for food.

(Following pages) Sunset shows through a tiny gap in the clouds over Pigeon Point Lighthouse.

(Third following page) Crescent City Lighthouse sits atop a wave-pounded, rocky cape.

(Preceding page, above) Wildflowers brighten the Coast just south of Big Sur, with the typical Big Sur fog lying just offshore.

(Preceding page, below) Gathering clouds hint at a change in the weather for this land-, sea- and skyscape near Carpenteria.

(Opposite) Sea stacks—rocky islands—are visible through the pines near Crescent City.

(Right) Peaceful inland lakes and lagoons nurture a colorful population of water-lilies.

(Below) The sea stacks near Crescent City are probably remnants of a prehistoric cape which has not yet totally yielded to the pounding of the waves.

(Following page) Shaped by wind and weather, a gaunt old cypress faces another sunset at Point Lobos, south of Carmel.

(Second following page, above) Southern Californians' love for pleasure boats is apparent in this view of the crowded Santa Barbara Yacht Harbor.

(Second following page, below) Late afternoon sun highlights the weathered brow of Point Lobos, at Point Lobos State Park.

(Third following page, above) Houses stand as close to the ocean as possible on the beach at Malibu; the towers of Los Angeles are visible in the background.

(Third following page, below) Hidden Beach is a short, sandy expanse on the Coast Trail in Redwood National Park.

eventually gathering enough public support for the state to establish redwood parks.

The magnificence of a virgin redwood forest seldom fails to impress visitors. Prairie Creek State Park, the first and biggest of the preserves north of Eureka, presently covers 13,000 acres on the coastal and inland sides of the Redwood Highway. The seashore aspect of the park is a wilderness forest wonderland. (Actually, the entire park is wholly natural except for some forty miles of trails and the Redwood Highway that runs through it). A herd of Roosevelt elk roams this forest-girt seashore on lower Redwood Creek. Here the dense summer fogs and heavy winter rains foster a lush growth of vegetation on the scale of a rain forest. Within its vast embrace is another of those fern canyons, this one notable for its perfectly sheer walls completely covered with ferns, and for its level, pebbly floor that invites an easy hike through it. The delicious sense of identity with nature fostered by such a walk is hard to describe or surpass.

North of the park one of the great rivers of California, the Klamath, gives its waters to the ocean. The river figures in not only the north coast's logging and mining story but in Indian history, too. It begins over the border in southern Oregon at Upper Klamath Lake and is 263 miles long in California, making it the state's second longest river. Nearly 200 miles to its mouth are free of dams, which means it's a good place to be, from the salmon and steelhead point of view. The Yurok Indians prospered for a long time by the Klamath estuary, partaking of its abundance and that of the ocean. The first white men were the gold-hunting mobs, the Forty-Niners who cut a bloody and devastating swath through the region. The Klamath has had all it can do to maintain its reputation as a great angling stream against disturbance of its watershed by logging and mining.

Scenic drives off Highway 101 skirt the cliffs high above the beach, up to the vicinity of Crescent City. One of the spectacular sights is the grandiose gorge the Klamath River cuts where it enters the Pacific. Where the roads circle back of the curving headlands, spurs lead down to the beaches, to the headlands, and to communities on the big river. The terrible winter floods of 1964 on the Klamath River wrought tremendous damage along the lower river, destroying towns and resorts. Some, such as Klamath, have been rebuilt since then on higher ground. At Requa, just off the main highway, a scenic road climbs high onto the headland north of the estuary, opening up dazzling river and ocean vistas that seem almost unreal.

The Redwood Highway runs low along the sandy beach on its way to Crescent City, but climbs high again during a nine-mile trip through Del Norte Redwoods

(Preceding page) Hearst Castle, at San Simeon, was once the home of newspaper magnate William Randolph Hearst.

State Park. Crescent City and its crescent bay were reputedly discovered by friends of a dying gold prospector who told of a fabulous hoard he had hidden in the Smith River drainage. The town was settled in the late 1850s and quickly became a busy port for mining ores from southwest Oregon. But lumber pushed everything else into the background by 1870. The success of Crescent City as a shipper of lumber and other materials was assured by its favorable coastal configuration. But it is not immune from ocean-borne destruction. In 1964 a seismic wave devastated the business district and took 11 lives. Offshore islands and rock structures enhance the beauty of the shoreline profile. Point St. George is just north of town, shielding city and bay from the strong north winds.

Jedediah Smith has things pretty well locked up in the Crescent City country and on up to the border. Starting at the town there is the Smith River Plain, then in about ten more miles the Smith River itself (or at least its mouth). East and north of the town is the Jedediah Smith Redwoods State Park, entered by US 199, which branches off from the coast road north of town. One tree in this grove is 340 feet high and 20 feet through. The Smith River is a salmon and steelhead stream that rivals even the Klamath, whose fishing resources have already been noted. The Smith is, in addition, known for its extraordinary green waters. The migrating fish arrive in the river during October and November. Then the estuary waters and lower river banks sprout fishermen in such numbers you might marvel at the skill and determination of the fish that gets upstream to spawn.

(Following page, above) Fishing boats lie at anchor in Monterey Harbor.
(Following page, below) The rocky Big Sur coastline offers scant foothold for vegetation.

The Sandy, Saintly Coastline

San Francisco, Santa Cruz, San Luis Obispo, Santa Maria, Santa Barbara, Los Angeles, San Clemente, San Diego—the names of a lot of Southern California's big coastal towns read like a roster of the heavenly elect, or at the very least a list of nominees for eternal beatitude. The Spanish did well to invoke the cooperation of the biblical blessed in connection with many of the beautiful Latin place names of Southern California's coast. The names seem especially appropriate to the almost unearthly glory of this sun-splashed shoreline.

It is more heavily settled than the northern reaches, but there are still places where nature at least has the upper hand, while accommodating human establishments of appropriate scale and appearance. The ocean side of the San Francisco peninsula still retains its rural personality in contrast to the string cities of the Bay. California Highway 1 begins to take up its coastal mode again after passing San Pedro Point south of Pacifica, the last big town for awhile. It sweeps close to the sea and around the base of the peninsula, touching close to the white sands of Half Moon Bay. From San Pedro Point, past Half Moon Bay and down to Monterey Bay the coastal valleys are bathed in cooling fog in summer and rain during the mild winters. For that reason they have become the prime region in the country for growing artichokes. The fertile soil is carpeted with the spiky, silvery-green plants in the spring and summer, and they are harvested the rest of the year.

On the way to Half Moon Bay, State Highway 1 climbs over highlands above San Pedro Point, giving the traveler access to widely assorted views of the Bay Area on the north and east. Set against the ocean and the Bay, near and distant peaks of land rise into the field of vision. Across the Golden Gate, Mount Tamalpais and Point Reyes can be seen. Even the Farallon Islands, 30 miles offshore from the Golden Gate's Point Bonita, project their rocky profiles through the sea mist. But the business at hand is Half Moon Bay. The arc-shaped bay, with a submerged reef protecting its waters, was a frequent port of call in times past for whalers and trading ships, some of which, during Prohibition, were engaged in a little funny business.

For a number of miles after the bay the coast is characterized by sandy bluffs bordering the surf. Then pine-covered mountains take over, almost shouldering the highway into the sea with their pushy presence close to surf's edge. Later the beach

(Preceding page) Swimmers and strollers enjoy this beach, tucked between rocky promontories at La Jolla.

widens and the road takes the cliff route around it. State parks follow each other along the bay's wide arc like so many links in a chain.

Around the northern curve of the bay the broad Pajaro Valley specializes in apple orchards, which turn into a fragrant white bower in the springtime and a vivid green one in the summer. Watsonville sits enthroned along the Pajaro River about five miles back from the bay. The smallish town is the apple and strawberry distribution center for the valley.

The dreamlike Monterey Peninsula stands out from the southern arm of the big crescent bay with a justifiable show of importance. The peninsula area is exemplary of the good life, first under Spanish auspices, then American. The town of Monterey, on the northern neck of the peninsula, was briefly the capital of California when the state was admitted to the union in 1850. It's still the "capital" of the Monterey country, which may be enough distinction, because there never was another country like it. The climate is benign throughout the year—in the sixties in summer, the fifties in winter. There's lots of sunshine, even during the wettest month (January).

Even though Monterey, Pacific Grove, and Carmel attract a lot of tourists, they have escaped becoming "touristy." The relaxed, comfortable pace they offer is just what comes naturally, with or without the visitors. Monterey's famous old Fisherman's Wharf is still almost as much a fishing pier as when it was built in 1846. Although dwindling catches have reduced the importance of fishing for Monterey, John Steinbeck's novels have bestowed a kind of immortality on its cannery area. Now the wharf area features gift shops and restaurants that cater to visitors, but the essential delicious, unhurried tempo still casts a hypnotic spell. Traditions are treated with loving care. Monterey has carefully preserved them in its historic buildings, some dating from the Spanish period.

Like Monterey, Pacific Grove is a peninsular town where history is visible, although the architectural examples of it are more recent. The Victorian houses on the bayside reflect, perhaps, not only a building style, but an entire life style, at least in early-day Pacific Grove, when decorum was mandated and the blue laws were more numerous than the sea gulls. Pacific Grove is still very much a family place, with delicious beaches, playgrounds, and cultural attractions. Pine, willow, and eucalyptus trees provide a green accent to the little town, and every October draw millions of migrating Monarch butterflies from east of the Rockies and from British Columbia. The butterflies presumably get "high" on the nectar of the trees, an unusual condition in Pacific Grove, which is "dry" for everyone else.

The ocean side of the peninsula has its rocky shores and pounding surf. Great

(Following page) Sunset washes a lonely stretch of Agate Beach with color.

sand dunes line the beach edges at Asilomar, a resort and convention center just outside of Pacific Grove. South of here the famed 17-Mile Drive of the peninsula runs past a beach of brilliant white sand. Cypress Point and some other promontories that delineate the south coast of Monterey Peninsula are in the much-photographed category, by reason of their dramatic meetings with the sea and their weirdly beautiful, tortured-looking Monterey cypress trees. The wild surf foams and sprays high into the air in its ceaseless battering of the steep cliffs and rocky inlets. All of these elements—the angry ocean and stark bluffs crowned by grotesquely twisted cypress trees—have a surreal impact that remains for a long time with anyone who sees and hears their thrilling drama.

The Monterey cypress has no lock on the appreciative sense of flora and fauna fanciers. The 17-Mile Drive affords access to so many plant and animal varieties, the drive would have to be a walk for visitors to see it all. Several cypress species on the peninsula demand one's attention, along with pines and other varieties of arboreal life. Offshore islands harbor sea lions, seals, and sea birds in such numbers that fights develop over territory. The sea otter, once thought to have been hunted to extinction along California, is once again in residence.

Much of the southern half of the peninsula is a masterpiece of cooperation between man and nature, a private enclave with public access limited. The famous Del Monte Forest is run like a laboratory by the owners, with no hunting allowed and strict limitations on public use areas. The natural balance is maintained by constant supervision; the public is in a sense on the outside, looking in. Carmel, the artist's village at the peninsula's southern base, is, of course, public, but it woos visitors on its own terms. Carmel was, first and foremost, a mission settlement; the Carmel Mission was founded in 1771 by the tireless Father Serra. The church and other mission buildings have been carefully preserved, and hardly anyone who visits Carmel leaves without making a pilgrimage there. The curving beaches of Carmel are among the world's most beautiful, but the cold waters of the bay are best left to the seals and sea lions.

The southern end of Carmel Bay is another spectacular landmark along the California coast. Point Lobos is a big, rocky peninsula, now a state preserve. It is driveable all the way out to the headland, but the most interesting recesses are reached only by foot paths. Some of the trails lead along the steep cliffs out to viewpoints fronting the sea and overlooking the playing sea lions. The combination of pine forests, windswept rocky heights, salt air, oceanic roar, and sun (especially the

(Following page, above) The quiet town of Mendocino seems to preserve a lifestyle from times past.
(Following page, below) Waves take on interesting formations where the current of the Klamath River meets the sea.

setting sun) is indeed a heady one. On the south shore are some coves with calm waters and tide pools crowded with sea life.

The Big Sur coastline gives away nothing in wild beauty to any part of California's shore. State Highway 1 follows close to its ragged cliffs, high above the angry spray and backed up by the long Santa Lucia Range. Just driving along the coastal road is adventure enough as it soars on lofty bridges above canyons where the mountains open up to the sea. Further adventures are available on side roads that wind down to the shore or into the mountains. Viewpoints along the way offer heart-stopping glimpses of a still-mysterious shoreline that seems even more eerie when the fog creeps into a coastal canyon below you, sealing it off from the rest of the world.

It seems beyond belief that the Big Sur coast remains so wild when a few hundred miles to the south people and their artifacts are jostling each other for space. But the Big Sur country is still about as it was in the beginnings of human settlement—a bleak, inhospitable land-seascape whose relatively few inhabitants are independent, lonely types who fit in well with their setting. The road along some of the wilder shores has to hug the cliffs where the mountains leave no room for a coastal shelf. When the Santa Lucias finally move back a little, at San Simeon, they are still center stage, in a sense. Here, on the mountain slopes a few miles back of the coast, is the Arabian Nights estate of William Randolph Hearst. For sheer ostentation it beats most any other private dwelling put together by man. The State of California maintains it as the Hearst San Simeon Historical Monument, open to the public for an admission fee.

Morro Bay is a small fishing and tourist town down the road near San Luis Obispo. The bay of Morro Bay is really a landlocked lagoon, and the town looks down on it from a bluff. The biggest single piece of the scenery is Morro Rock, an immense volcanic pile that rises out of the bay to a height of 576 feet. Morro Rock is one of a chain of old volcanoes, the rest of which can be seen from State 1 as it turns away from the coastal bulge on its way to San Luis Obispo, another town that grew up around one of Father Serra's missions (San Luis Obispo de Tolosa).

The shoreline road unites briefly with US 101, which comes out momentarily to the coast around the southern end of the Santa Lucias before retreating again to the back country. The big bulge of California between San Luis Obispo and Santa Barbara is still pleasantly uncrowded, although not exactly deserted. The beach towns at the north end, like Pismo Beach, are rather well trod during the summer. Others, like Oceano, are still able to provide beach solitude. When it's not being a flower-seed

(Following page, above) Dusk falls over the Golden Gate as the setting sun fills the sky with color.
(Following page, below) A single boat moves through the stillness of early morning fog in the Santa Barbara Harbor.

growing and vegetable farming area, this mesaland is taken up with military matters. Vandenberg Air Force Base occupies a vast coastal tract. The big towns are Lompoc and Santa Maria, making their living from the fertile valley soils.

The main roads avoid the coast until they get around to the Santa Barbara side; then State 1 and US 101 come together and visit the incurving shoreline of the Santa Barbara Channel. The Santa Inez Mountains rise very close to the shoreline, leaving the highway only a narrow passage above the surf as far as Goleta, a few miles west of Santa Barbara. As anyone knows who has visited Santa Barbara, this is one of the loveliest towns on any coast. Its setting and climate have been compared to the *Cote d' Azur* of the Mediterranean.

The conformation of the Santa Inez Mountains here is something like an amphitheater. Santa Barbara rises gently up from its little crescent harbor into the lower mountain slopes. The sheltering ridges contribute to the area's gentle climate. Much of the town was rebuilt after the earthquake of 1925, with careful attention to architectural themes reflecting its Spanish heritage. The contiguous areas of Montecito on the east flank, and Hope Ranch on the west, hide luxurious homes in their lemon groves.

Somewhere south of Santa Barbara begins an entirely different chapter in the story of the California coast. Here the world's biggest and most spectacular natural feature—the Pacific Ocean—laps at the edge of one of the world's biggest and most spectacular urban areas: Greater Los Angeles. Taken with a liberal dose of sunshine and some big waves, this massive coincidence of nature and humanity is a phenomenon all by itself. The first American surfing was done at Redondo Beach in 1907 by George Douglas Freeth, imported from Hawaii by promoters of the Hotel Redondo. The rest, as they say, is history.

Topographically this portion of the southern California coast lends itself to beaches. The Santa Monica Mountains stand far enough back from the ocean to allow beaches from Malibu southwards in a giant crescent to the Palos Verdes Peninsula. Where there are no mountains, the land ends in gentle headlands of varying heights above the sands, and beach-towns crowd the brink. The Palos Verdes Peninsula is taken up with fine homes, tree-shaded streets, riding trails and some cliff-hanging houses on its upper reaches. Then comes the Long Beach-to-San Diego sweep, a much larger crescent which offers more open and sunny beaches, and some sheltered coves formed by low-lying but rocky headlands.

Twenty-seven miles offshore are the Channel Islands, the most popular of which is Santa Catalina. Avalon, its single town, though very touristy, has no traffic

(Preceding page) Wildflowers find sustenance on rocks near the water's edge at Big Sur.

problem because visitors can't bring their cars. For the most part the land has been held in trust by the Wrigley family, and the result has been to preserve a delicious ambiance reminiscent of the Southern California of 30 or 40 years ago.

More of this ambiance is accessible as the beaches make their smooth southward sweep to San Diego and the Mexican border. The seashore continues more or less unbroken, sometimes broad and sandy, in other places narrow and backed by steep headlands, squeezed almost out of existence in a few picturesque places where rocky bluffs wet their feet in the ocean. Towns like Laguna Beach and San Clemente, outside of Los Angeles' sphere of influence, resemble more the tropical towns that they really are, making concessions to the increased pace of progress without being lost in it. South of Camp Pendleton at Oceanside, a county road leaves the freeway for a really close look at the ocean, and access to a number of state beaches, and it's possible to follow this road clear to Mission Bay Park in San Diego.

With Los Angeles occupying public eye, cussed and discussed through the media, there isn't a great deal of mention of its neighbor to the south, the great and growing city of San Diego. Beginning with one of Father Serra's missions (San Diego de Alcala) the town has quietly and gracefully grown into one of the nation's top ten in terms of population. Blessed with plenty of frontage on the ocean and San Diego Bay, including a beautiful harbor abounding in pleasure craft, San Diego offers a variety of treats to those folks who take their ocean with a dash of city.

And south of San Diego—five miles from Coronado, more or less—is Border Field State Park, the very end of the 1,200 miles that make up the California coast. It's a place some people will want to go just to be able to say they've been there.

(Following page) This somber sunset displays one of the infinite moods of the Southern California coast.